How to make
Paper Candle-Shades

Polly Pinder

Search Press

First published in Great Britain 1994

Search Press Limited
Wellwood, North Farm Road,
Tunbridge Wells, Kent TN2 3DR

Text and illustrations copyright © Polly Pinder 1994

Photography by Search Press Studio
Photography copyright © Search Press 1994

ISBN 0 85532 781 2

Printed in Spain by Elkar S. Coop, 48012, Bilbao.

Safety Notice

I cannot over-emphasise the care that should be taken when using candles. If the following precautions are taken the shades will be perfectly safe:

1. Use only the small candles which sit in a little metal case – these can be bought quite cheaply at some craft shops or shops which specialise in oriental products.

2. Never use a candle alone; always put it in a clear, thick glass jar which is taller than the flame – this will prevent danger from draughts. Neat little jars can usually be purchased from the same source as the candles.

3. Never leave a lighted candle and shade unattended, and certainly never within the reach of a curious child.

Contents

Introduction

The first paper lanterns were probably made in China, where paper itself was invented around the second century BC. Many early oriental paintings depict the use of lanterns in everyday use or for special ceremonies and festivals. The gentle flickering light of a candle gives a lovely sense of intimacy and comfort, either as the focal point of the dinner table or brightening some dark corner of the room.

In this book I show you how to make candle-shades from a wide range of materials that can be used to complement a variety of moods and occasions. None are really difficult to make – most being relatively simple in design – but some do require more delicate craftsmanship and patience than others.

I firmly believe that we all have untapped potential. I hope my examples will inspire you to experiment: to use the wonderful variety of materials that are available to good effect, and to create your own unique designs.

Materials

Paper for the shades should be neither so thick as to prevent the light from coming through nor so thin that the shade cannot stand unaided. If a paper does seem too weak (a typing or photocopy paper for example) a band of slightly thicker paper, stuck round the top and bottom edges, will help to secure its structure. Almost any paper which fulfils these two criteria can be used: white or pastel-coloured cartridge, textured writing paper or handmade papers. I have included drafting film, acetate and coloured cellophane because their translucent or transparent qualities mean that they lend themselves perfectly to uses with light. Handmade papers can be bought at specialist paper merchants. They often provide a mail order service and will (for a nominal fee) send a comprehensive collection of small samples. If you have difficulty finding one try contacting the art/design department of your college; they may be able to help. Alternatively, you could try making your own – there are lots of books on this subject and details of some are included at the back of this book.

Adhesives

Gluing is often a matter of personal preference. I used double-sided sticky tape (referred to in the text as DSST) to join the seams of the shades and a recently introduced dry adhesive, which comes in sheet form, to stick shapes to the walls of the shades. You will also need some ordinary sticky tape. I do use low-tack tape during the production of some shades to prevent damage to the paper (alternatively you could rub most of the tackiness from some masking tape).

Tools

A specific list of materials and equipment is given with the step-by-step instructions for each shade but you will need the following basic tools: a cutting mat or piece of heavy card; a steel-edged ruler; a craft knife and some sharp blades; a pair of sharp-pointed scissors; 2H and HB pencils; pencil sharpener (always have a sharp point); and an eraser.

Simple paper shades

Indian or Japanese handmade paper gives such a lovely and interesting effect that it needs no other ornament or decoration. The papers are made from diverse natural materials: jute, straw, flowers, hemp, banana leaves, husks or even algae; they come in different weights (thickness) and finishes (rough and smooth).

The perforated design (opposite) is an adaptation of a simple tubular shade. Any shapes can be cut from the paper, so long as the structure of the shade is not weakened. I chose this one because the paper has a fine diagonal indentation. The cut-out strips are at right angles to the indentations. As the paper was rather thin I added strengthening circles at the top and bottom.

Making shades

Cut an accurate rectangle which will fit comfortably round the small candle jar mentioned in the introduction, or a jam jar. Stick a strip of DSST down one edge and join the two sides together. Do this carefully to prevent creasing the paper (practise with some cheap paper first). If you have a firm cylinder to hand, a thick rolling pin for example, use it as a support so that pressure can be applied to the join without the risk of permanently distorting the shade.

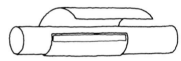

You can adapt the basic design by introducing cut-out shapes. Make sure that the cut-outs are balanced at the top and bottom, i.e. avoid part-shapes, and make the bottom border slightly deeper than the top one; if they are equal, the bottom border will appear to be narrower.

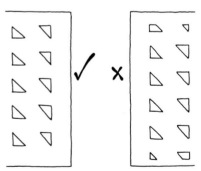

I generally prefer diffused light rather than a visible flame and I used a full lining of drafting film on this shade. The sheet of drafting film should be the same width as the paper and about 3–4mm (1/8in) shorter in length. Slip the lining inside the shade, matching the two seams. The lining should fit snugly against the shade; there is no need to stick them together.

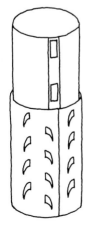

Food cans

These are strictly 'fun' shades which could be used for an informal supper or, if you dare, a very formal dinner party where the table settings and decorations are laid to perfection, then you light the candles and say apologetically that you will be eating the contents of the tins for dinner. . .

To make the food can shades you will need: labels from various food cans (pet food included); white photocopy paper; a silver felt-tipped pen; and the equipment given on page 4.

Making food-can shades

1. Carefully remove the label from the can. If there are any ugly blobs of dried glue left on the label, chip or scrape them off with your craft knife. Trim away uneven edges.

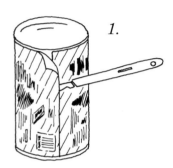

1.

2. Cut the white paper 6mm (¹/₄in) deeper and 3mm (¹/₈in) longer than the label. Draw a silver line, approximately 3mm (¹/₈in) wide along the top and bottom edges of the paper. Turn the paper over and draw two similar lines on the other side.

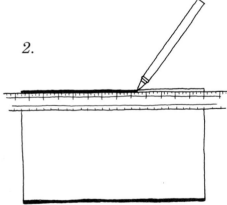

2.

3. Using a thin strip of DSST stick the label, face down, to one of the shorter edges of the white paper, leaving the two silver lines exposed. Attach another strip of DSST to the label, as shown, then turn the two over and attach a further strip of tape, the full depth of the white paper.

3.

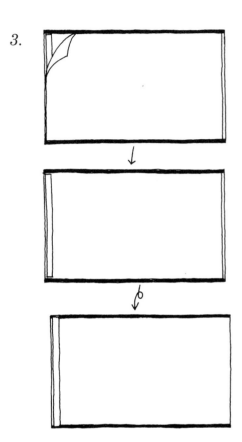

4. It is important that the white paper lies as close to the label as possible, otherwise the image on the label becomes blurred. Curl the label round and stick one side on top of the other as shown on page 7. Curl the white paper round the outside, pulling as tightly as possible, and stick the ends together.

4.

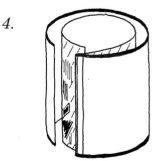

9

Stamp shades

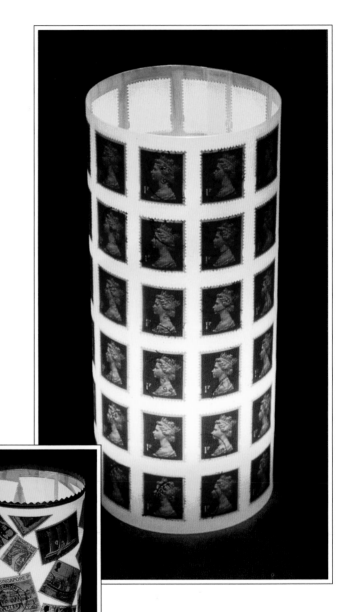

This is a good way of using old stamps, particularly after the annual deluge of Christmas cards. Irregular-sized stamps can be applied to the shade at random – although this implies minimal planning, it is important that the arrangement of stamps is decided before sticking them down. Sixty stamps, all of the same size, were used for the formal design in six rows of ten. I left 6mm (¹/₄in) gaps between each stamp, a border of 6mm (¹/₄in) round three sides and a 12mm (¹/₂in) border down the right side for the join. Both shades have a drafting-film cover to diffuse the light.

To make the stamp shades you will need: an A4 (8¹/₄ x 12in) sheet each of clear or tinted acetate, clear adhesive-backed film and drafting film; two A4 (8¹/₄ x 12in) sheets of white paper; some graph paper (for formal design); selection of stamps; thick black felt-tipped pen; a pair of pinking shears; and the equipment given on page 4.

Removing stamps from envelopes

1. Soak the stamps in water for about thirty minutes. The pieces of envelope will separate from the stamps. Remove the pieces of envelope. While the stamps are still in the water rub the back of each one with your fingers to remove glue.

2. Lay the stamps between a double thickness of kitchen towel and place something heavy on top – a bread board and a couple of books for example. Leave overnight or until perfectly dry. You will need to replace the paper towels once.

Foreign paper money could be used in much the same way as stamps. A wider shade would be needed (housing two or three candles) to accommodate the greater size of notes. The fact that paper currency is printed on both sides will add to the effect rather than diminish it. If the notes are crumpled or creased, iron them under a damp cloth before attaching them to the adhesive film.

Making the shade

1. Using the black felt-tipped marker, draw a line 6mm ($^1/_4$in) deep along the top and bottom edges of the drafting film. When the ink has dried carefully trim with your pinking shears, keeping as close to the edge as possible.

2. Cut 6mm ($^1/_4$in) from the top and one side edge of both pieces of white paper.

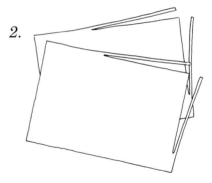

3. Now draw pencil guide lines on both sheets: two at the top and bottom, 6mm ($^1/_4$in) in from the edge; one 12mm ($^1/_2$in) in from the right side; and another 3mm ($^1/_8$in) in from the left.

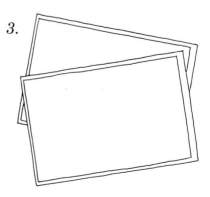

4. For the random design use one of the papers to arrange the stamps; cut them as necessary to get straight lines on all four edges. For the formal design draw a grid on the graph paper.

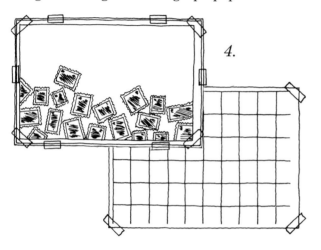

4.

6.

7. Attach a strip of DSST to the 12mm (¹/₂in) border, curl the shade round (stamps facing out) and stick the two sides together.

7.

5. Attach the second sheet of white paper or the graph paper to your cutting mat. Position the piece of clear adhesive-backed film, sticky side up, over the paper and carefully transfer each stamp from the loose arrangement.

5.

6. When all the stamps have been stuck down lay the piece of acetate on top. Firmly rub between and over the stamps with a soft cloth. Using the edges of the paper as a guide, cut out the shade leaving surplus acetate and adhesive-backed film.

8. The drafting-film cover should be approximately 6mm (¹/₄in) wider than the shade. To ensure a snug fit, wrap it round the shade and mark the overlap. Attach DSST on the overlap and stick the sides together. Slide the shade into the cover (you may have to carefully squash the shade to get started).

8.

Autumn-leaf shade

This very pretty shade is made much in the same way as the stamp shades, except that the drafting film is placed on the inside and a sheet of tissue paper is used to cover the leaves.

Gather some autumn leaves and press them immediately between sheets of newspaper under a pile of books. They can be used as soon as they are completely dry. I used an Indian handmade tissue paper for this shade, which, when lit from behind, shows its delicate cotton fibres – but any type of semi-transparent paper will do.

To make the autumn-leaf shade you will need: several leaves; a piece of clear adhesive-backed film; a piece of drafting film; and the equipment given on page 4.

Note I have not specified sizes for the clear adhesive-backed film and drafting film as they depend on the arrangement of leaves; the shade illustrated measures 200 x 330mm (8 x 13in).

Embossed shade

Embossing creates one of the subtlest images for a candle-shade. Watercolour paper is used because its composition makes it a perfect medium for stretching. The thicker the paper, the clearer and stronger the embossed image but of course if the paper is too thick the candlelight is unable to penetrate. If the paper is too thin it will tear during the embossing process. I have used 90lb (190gsm) paper, which, if handled carefully, will not rip. It also allows just enough light for the image to be seen.

Initials make a good subject for embossing. For the shade pictured here I took a P and a J from a script typeface and extended the lines so that the two became entwined. You could write a message or an old proverb along the top of the shade or even diagonally round it. Alternatively you may want to fill the whole area with words – there are many possibilities. The images do not have to be composed of letters – you could try a simple scene or an object – but because they are linear, letters do lend themselves to the embossing technique. A wonderful collection of alphabet designs can be found in catalogues (usually available from art and craft shops) or in specific alphabet design books from the library.

To make the embossed shade you will need: a sheet of plain paper; some tracing paper; a sheet, roughly 280 x 380mm (11 x 15in), of 190gsm (90lb) watercolour paper; a 230 x 330mm (10 x 13in) piece of white card 1mm (¹/₁₆in) thick; a burnishing tool (this can be plastic, metal or bone and is available from art and craft shops); and the equipment given on page 4.

Making the shade

For this exercise I have used the numerals 1 and 8, to show how to deal with 'counters' (the enclosed shapes within some characters).

1. When you have finalised your design, trace it on to the card so that the image on the card is the wrong way round.

1.

2. Place the card on your cutting mat and, using your craft knife and a new blade, carefully cut the image out. Your letter or design may be such that you are left with two or three 'counters' (the middle pieces from the number eight in this case).

2.

3. Turn the card over so that the image is the right way round, and position the counters in exactly the same place as the original design; carefully place pieces of sticky tape to secure them.

3.

4. Turn the card over again and put more pieces of tape over the first ones, but this time, press the tape into the sides of the cut-out – see the diagram. The tape underneath should lie flat while that which you have just secured should follow the shape of the design.

4.

Press the tape down the sides of the cut-out

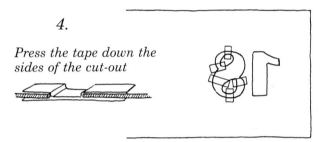

5. This step will have to be done during daylight hours, unless you have a light box. Stick the card, wrong way facing, on to a window, at a height where you can work comfortably and then stick the watercolour paper over the card. Using your burnishing tool and gentle pressure, follow the outline of the design, stretching the paper down into the relief image in the card. As you burnish the design lift two corners of the paper and check to see that the embossing is working.

5.

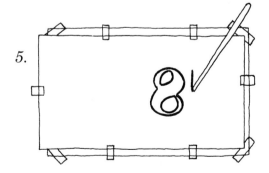

6. When you are satisfied with the result remove the paper and card from the window. The shade can be of any size, provided that it will fit over the candle holder. Trim the paper to the required size, attach a strip of DSST to one of the side edges, curl the shade round and stick together as shown on page 7.

x-resist shades

Here are two shades created using the wax-resist method. The hexagonal green blotched shade is made from an Indian handmade tissue paper which can be bought at specialist paper shops. It is tougher and denser than the commercial tissue paper used for the cylindrical striped purple shade.

To make one of the wax-resist shades you will need: an A4 (8¹/₄ x 12in) sheet of tissue paper; a dish of house-hold bleach; a No. 8 paintbrush; some pieces of clean white paper; plenty of newspaper; a candle; an iron; a palette knife; and the equipment given on page 4.

Making the shades

1. Cut two strips, each 10mm (³/₈in) wide, from the long edge of the tissue paper. Attach pieces of DSST then leave on one side.

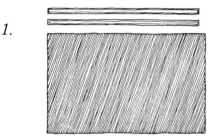

1.

2. Make a pad of newspaper, cover with white paper and lay the remaining sheet of tissue paper on top.

2.

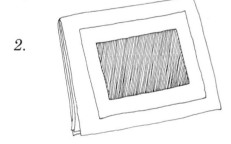

3. Tilt the lighted candle and let the wax drip on to the tissue. Before the drops have time to harden, smear them over the paper with the palette knife, leaving some areas clear. For the striped effect dribble the wax up and down the tissue. In order to get a solid line the candle needs to be held close to the tissue – take care not to singe it.

3.

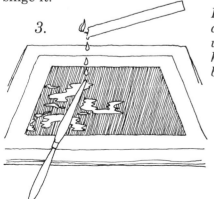

Drip the wax and smear with a palette knife for the blotched effect.

Dribble the wax up and down for the striped effect.

4. Brush bleach all over the surface then leave to soak in for a few minutes.

4.

5. Place the tissue on more sheets of newspaper. Put a folded sheet on top and carefully iron (the iron should be hot enough to melt the wax but not burn the paper!) Replace the newspaper which has absorbed the wax and iron again. Finally place the tissue between sheets of white paper and iron again.

5.

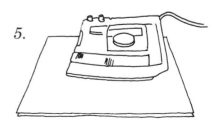

6. For the hexagonal shade only, trim the tissue to a length of 280mm (11in) and then mark 45mm

(1³⁄₄in) intervals along the length of the sheet, leaving 10mm (¹⁄₂in) at the end. Lay a steel-edged ruler against the marks and, using the blunt edge of your craft knife, lightly score six lines. Crease the score lines.

7. Carefully stick the two unbleached strips along the top and bottom edges of the tissue, trimming off any excess. For the hexagonal shade, lightly score the newly applied edges, following the existing score lines.

8. Stick a strip of DSST along the flap then join the two ends together. Shape the shade according to the design used (hexagonal or cylindrical).

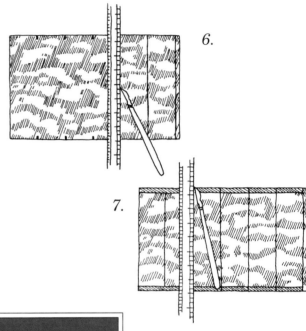

6.

7.

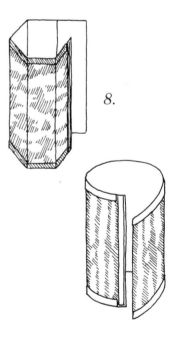

8.

The shades are rather delicate to handle but they are very attractive, both when illuminated by candlelight (see page 16) and in daylight.

Concertina shade

This shade was made with a parchment-type paper which can be bought from most art and craft shops. The paper is simply concertina-folded along its length and the end folds are joined with DSST.

Making the shade

Using a sharp pencil, lightly mark 20mm ($^3/_4$in) in from one side at the top and bottom (long) edges. Lay a rule against the marks, hold it down firmly and lift the paper to form a crease. Turn the paper over and make a crease in the other direction. Continue to turn and crease until the full concertina has been formed. You must end up with an even number of folds.

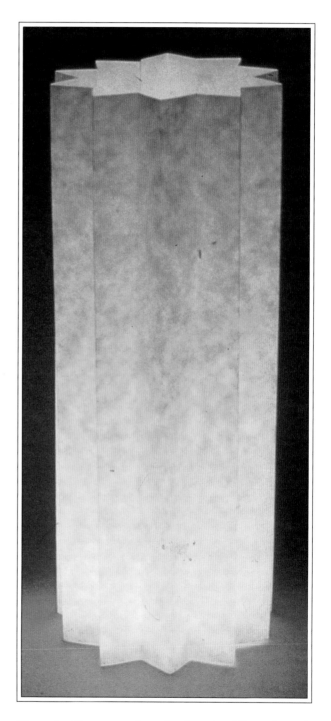

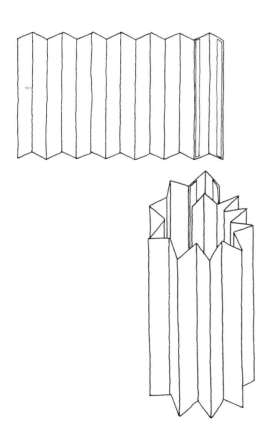

To make the concertina shade you will need a 250 x 400mm (10 x 15in) sheet of paper and some of the tools and adhesives given on page 4.

Chinese lanterns

I used a 'laid' paper for these shades and the glowing light gives a woody effect which, together with the slanting top, suggests a section of bamboo. Although the texture appears to be quite strong, the finish of the paper is in fact very smooth. Chinese calligraphy is exquisite in its perfectly controlled but seemingly spontaneous brush strokes. I use the shades at Chinese dinner parties and hope that my guests are 'charmed' enough not to notice the foil take-away dishes in the waste bin.

Each of the symbols shown denotes a charm.

1. Chao Ts'ai Chin Pao *is a charm to bring luck.*
2. Fu Shuang Ch'iian *is a charm to ensure prosperity and long life.*
3. Huang Chin Wan *will bring ten thousand ounces of gold.*

To make one lantern you will need: A4 (8¹/₄ x 12in) sheet of paper; a pair of compasses; a black felt-tipped marker with a brush tip; tracing paper; masking tape or some other low-tack adhesive tape; and the equipment given on page 4.

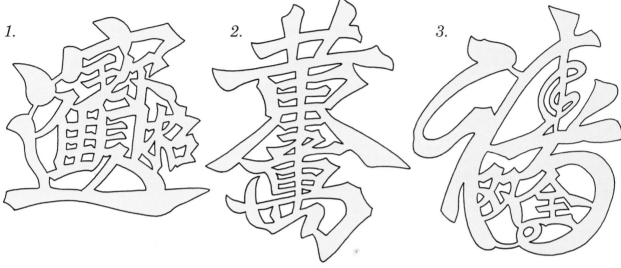

1. 2. 3.

Making Chinese lanterns

1. Cut a 20mm (³/₄in) strip from the long edge of the paper. Stick a piece of DSST along the strip.

1.

2. Trim the length of the remaining rectangle to 280mm (11in). Mark the middle of the long edge of the rectangle and then make a pencil mark 15mm (just under ⁵/₈in) in from one edge. Position the compass on that point and draw an arc which almost reaches the top of the rectangle. Carefully cut along this line using scissors or your craft knife – whichever you are more confident with. Rub out the pencil marks.

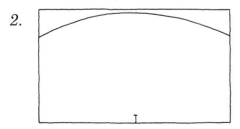

2.

3. Carefully trace a charm on to the shade paper. Use low-tack tape when securing the tracing paper to avoid damaging the shade. Using the brush pen, fill in the lines.

3.

4. Turn the paper over and stick a strip of DSST down the right side. Curl the paper round and stick the two sides together (see page 7). Matching the back seam, attach the strip of paper round the base of the shade. You may have to trim off a fraction at the end.

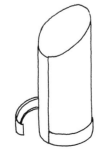

4.

Simple twisted lantern

The idea for this shade obviously comes from the little paper lanterns made at school during the pre-Christmas craft lessons. When I was sketching ideas for the shade I thought of many ways of introducing colour and pattern. However, when the mock-up was complete I thought that the light and gently twisting lines of paper epitomised the concept of design simplicity.

Glancing over the instructions for this shade you may think that a degree in mathematics would help. In fact it really is very simple, but accuracy is important in the measuring and cutting. Please note that the metric and imperial measurements are not interchangeable.

To make the twisted lantern you will need: 220 x 287mm (8^1/$_2$ x 10^3/$_4$in) sheet of drafting film; 300 x 570mm (12 x 23in) sheet of fine (lightweight) tinted paper; and the equipment given on page 4. I only had an A3 (12 x 16^1/$_2$) sheet of pink paper so I had to extend it in order to draw the diagonal line (see step 1).

Making the shade

1. Draw a rectangle 230mm deep and 290mm wide (9 x 10^7/$_8$in) in the centre of your tinted paper. Draw a 15mm (^{5}/$_8$in) border along the top and bottom edges, extending the top right and bottom left lines to the edge of the paper – if your sheet of paper is not large enough stick two pieces of ordinary paper on as temporary extensions. Draw a 10mm (^{3}/$_8$in) border down the right side and stick a strip of DSST over this border – do not remove the backing. Working from the left-hand side of the rectangle, lightly mark 10mm (^{3}/$_8$in) intervals along the top and bottom border lines, right through to the edge of the paper.

1.

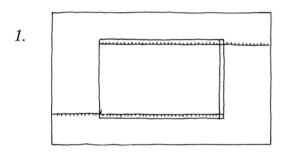

2. Starting 140mm (5^1/$_4$in) in from the top left-hand corner of the rectangle, draw a diagonal line down to the bottom left corner. Continue to draw diagonal lines (drawing over the DSST backing) to the right-hand edge of the rectangle. Go back and repeat at the other side. Cut the lines (cutting through the DSST) between the top and bottom borders. Stick a thin strip of DSST along the top border (do not remove backing) then carefully erase the border lines and interval marks.

2.

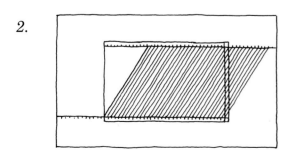

3. Stick a piece of DSST, 10mm (^{3}/$_8$in) wide, down the side of the drafting film, curl it round and join together to form the translucent lining.

3.

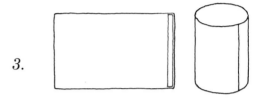

4. Carefully cut out the rectangle. Curl it round, remove the DSST backing (one piece at a time) and stick each corresponding strip together.

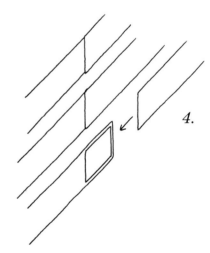

4.

5. When all the strips including the top and bottom borders have been stuck, carefully slide the lining up into the shade. Remove the backing from the strip of DSST at the top of the shade. Push the shade down to meet the top of the lining and stick the two tops together. The shade will now belly out.

5.

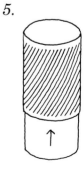

Painted lantern

Having designed and made the twisted lantern on page 22, I still wanted to try something similar but with added design. This shade was inspired by a fourteenth-century Chinese vase and is made from watercolour paper. If you find the idea of stretching and painting the watercolour paper too daunting, you could use a sturdy cartridge paper and blue felt-tipped pens.

I have included the design pattern that I used for this shade but it will have to be scaled up to size. You could of course create your own design.

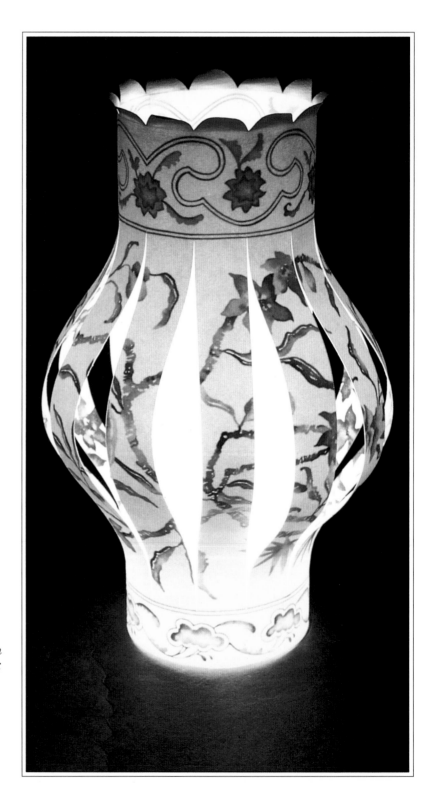

To make the painted lantern you will need: a 330 x 350mm (13 x 14in) sheet of 190gsm (90lb) watercolour paper; a 215 x 247mm (8$^1/_2$ x 9$^7/_8$in) sheet of drafting film; some tracing paper; a tube of blue watercolour paint; a No. 2 paintbrush; a large wooden (unvarnished) board and brown gummed parcel tape (for stretching the paper); and the equipment given on page 4.

Making the shade

1. Use a photocopier (or graph paper) to enlarge the design so that the full width of the pattern, including the overlap strip, is 250mm (10in). Trace the complete pattern including the vertical lines. Note that the image on the narrow strip at the left-hand side (the overlap) replicates that at the right-hand side of the main design to give a continuous pattern.

1.

2. Cut four pieces of gummed paper about 400mm (16in) long. Wet the watercolour paper by slipping it into a bowl or sink of water, gently shake off excess water and lay it on the board. Dampen the gummed paper and quickly stick down each edge of the watercolour paper. Bubbles will appear but as the paper dries it will become smooth and tight again.

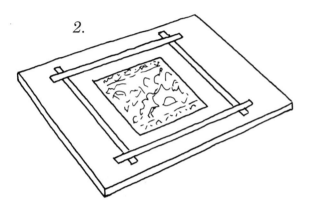

2.

3. When the paper is completely dry transfer the traced image on to the watercolour paper and then paint the design.

3.

Watercolours are different from gouache and poster paints. The idea is not to have solid, uniform areas of colour, but to allow the water to give varying densities of colour. The pencil lines are only a guide; it does not matter if your brush strays over or even if a flower does not resemble the initial drawing. Just try to aim for spontaneous, confident brush strokes which are not overworked. If you have never used watercolours before a little practice will help. Some of the lighter areas are achieved by mopping up excess paint with paper tissue or cotton-wool buds.

4. When the painting is dry, gently rub out the design pencil lines, taking care not to erase the vertical lines between the top and bottom borders. Remove the painting from the board then trim the side and bottom edges to size.

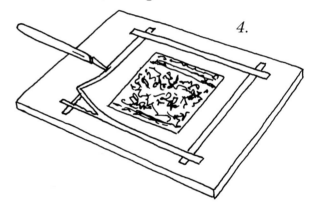

4.

5. Lay the painting on your cutting mat. Cut into the corners of the fluted top with your craft knife then carefully cut the curves with a pair of scissors.

5.

6. With the design facing down, stick a strip of DSST down the overlap flap. Turn the sheet over and stick a thin strip of DSST along the top edge, just below the points of the flutes – do not extend on to the overlap flap.

6.

7. Using your knife and steel-edged ruler, cut the vertical lines from the base of the top border to the top of the bottom border.

7.

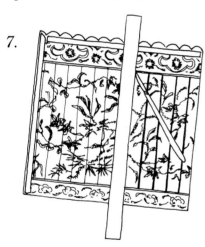

8. Using your knife handle or blunt edge of the scissors, curl each fluted top outwards.

8.

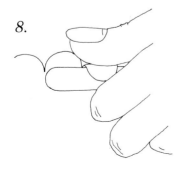

9. Curl the shade round and stick the two sides together. Stick a piece of DSST, 10mm ($^3/_8$in) wide, down one side of the drafting film. Curl it round and join together.

9.

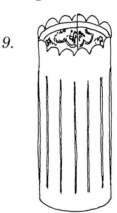

10. Remove the DSST backing along the fluted edge of the shade. Match the two seams and carefully push the lining up inside the shade. When the two bottom edges are aligned push the shade down so that the top of the lining sticks to the strip of DSST. The paper strips will now gently belly out.

10.

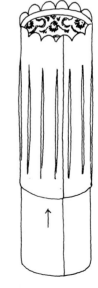

Bedroom shade

Paper doilies were cut up to provide the silhouette and decoration for this heart-shaped shade. I used gold doilies for the inside (they give a strong image) and the usual white doilies for the outside trimming at the top of the shade. The paper is slightly textured and fairly stiff.

Three candle jars fit neatly inside, two in the curves of the heart and one at the front. Doilies vary so much in size and shape that it is impossible to be exact about the final design; so use your skill and imagination to produce a pattern. (I find that doilies with circular sections are easier to manipulate.)

The only glue required for this shade (apart from DSST for the seam) is the dry adhesive sheets. It is expensive but very economical: nothing is wasted, you simply lay your cut-out on the glued sheet, rub firmly then lift and position on your paper.

To make this shade you will need: an A3 (12 x 16¹/₂in) sheet of paper; a packet each of gold and white doilies; a sheet of dry adhesive; a black felt-tipped pen; and the equipment given on page 4.

Making the shade

1. Trim the sheet of paper down to 250 x 420mm (10 x 16½in) then score it in half using the blunt edge of your knife. Stick a strip of DSST down one side. Turn the paper over and lightly draw a line down each side, the same width as the DSST.

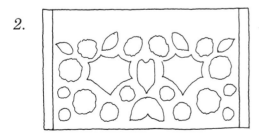

2. Having chosen your doilies, look to see which sections might produce an interesting design. Cut the gold pieces out and move them round until you get a good arrangement – avoid putting anything beyond the two pencil lines.

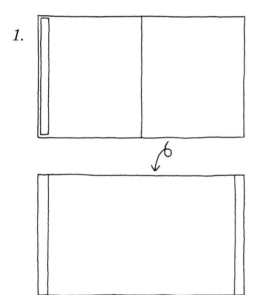

3. When the pieces are arranged to your liking, glue the white side to the paper. Using the black pen, join the sections together with small twig-like lines so that the design becomes one, rather than a collection of isolated pieces.

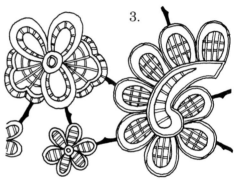

4. Turn the paper over. Arrange and stick white sections along the top edge. Carefully cut the edge, following the curved shapes formed by the sections.

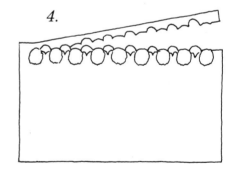

5. Carefully bend the paper round and stick the two sides together to form the shape of a heart.

Stained-glass shade

Coloured cellophane has been used to achieve the stained-glass effect in this three-sided shade. The process for making the shade is exacting – one needs to have dexterous hand-skills using the craft knife with very small pieces of cellophane and even smaller bits of DSST; patience is essential but this shade is well worth the effort.

To make the stained-glass shade you will need: sheets or rolls of coloured cellophane; an A3 (12 x 16¹/₂in) sheet each of sturdy black paper, drafting film and clear acetate; stick of white Conté crayon; an A4 (8¹/₄ x 12in) sheet of tracing paper; two similar-sized sheets of white paper; low-tack sticky tape; pair of compasses; fine black felt-tipped pen; and the equipment given on page 4.

Making the shade

1. Trace the full-size design then turn it over and rub Conté crayon over the pencil lines. Blow off excess dust. Attach the tracing, white side down, to the black paper, securing with low-tack tape. Trace the design.

1.

2. Remove the tracing and carefully cut out the whole shape out, scoring the flap with the blunt edge of your knife. I find it easier to cut free-hand, without a steel-edged rule (try this method on a spare piece of black paper).

2.

3. Carefully rub off any Conté crayon, turn the piece over on to a sheet of white paper and draw the design – this will be used as a cutting guide for the small pieces of cellophane.

3.

4. Tape a piece of acetate over the original tracing and using the felt-tipped pen draw a line inside the frame, 2mm ($^1/_8$in) larger than the design area. If you use a compass to draw the arc, make a small wad of several pieces of sticky tape and place it over the centre point; this prevents the compass needle from piercing the acetate.

4.

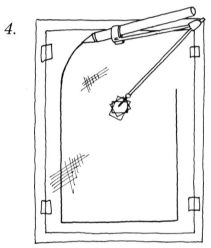

5. Remove the acetate and cut out the shape. With the reverse side of the black design facing, stick thin strips of DSST on the 'leading', then attach the acetate.

5.

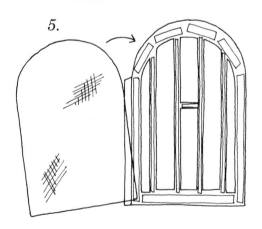

6. Stick the full width of DSST on to the acetate, cutting the top of each strip to follow the arc. Leave the backing on the DSST for the moment.

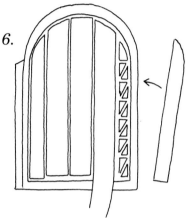

6.

7. Using the white paper cutting guide, lay pieces of cellophane over each section of the left strip, hold firmly and cut to fit. When all the pieces have been cut remove the backing from the left strip of DSST and carefully stick on each piece, burnishing it with your knife handle to remove any little air pockets. Continue in this manner until all the strips have been coloured. In order to achieve variation in density of colour, some sections will need another piece of the same colour. To apply these, cut thin strips of DSST and position round the section to be covered, then stick the cellophane on.

7.

8. Now the whole area needs to be covered with drafting film (to diffuse the light). Use the original tracing as a template and repeat step 4, making the film slightly larger. Stick thin strips of DSST along the leading again, then attach the drafting film.

8.

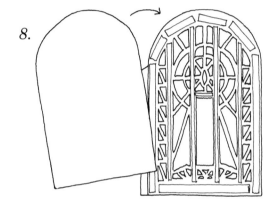

9. Repeat all the steps for the two remaining sides of the shade. Stick strips of DSST on to the flaps and join the three sides together.

9.

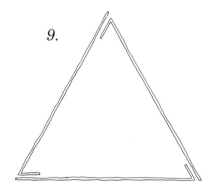

Chess shade

Serious chess players will probably wince at the position of these chess pieces, but as I have little knowledge of the game, they are arranged purely for aesthetic purposes. Please note that the metric and imperial measurements are not inter-changeable.

To make the chess shade you will need: an A3 (12 x 16¹/₂in) sheet each of parchment-type paper (available from most art and craft shops) and graph or ordinary white paper; a 220 x 380mm (9 x 15in) sheet of clear adhesive-backed film); some brown wrapping paper, roughly same size as the film; brown felt-tipped pen; and the equipment given on page 4.

Making the chess shade

1. Draw a grid on the graph or plain paper – thirty-two 40mm ($1^5/_8$in) squares (four rows of eight with a 1mm ($^1/_{16}$in) gap between each second column). Add a top and bottom border of 6mm ($^1/_4$in) and a side border of 10mm ($^3/_8$in). Extend the lines as shown on the diagram; they will be used as a guide for scoring, cutting and drawing the brown borders.

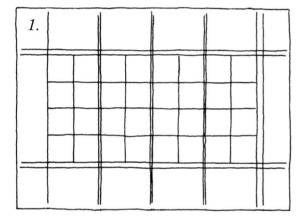

2. Draw about twenty 40mm ($1^5/_8$in) squares on to the brown paper and, using the full-size patterns, trace chess pieces on to most of them. Using your craft knife and a new blade carefully cut the pieces out of the squares. The cut-out pieces can go on to the blank white squares but if your cutting is a little shaky, concentrate on getting the brown squares right first, then draw the pieces separately and cut them out. It is surprising how adept you will become after a few squares.

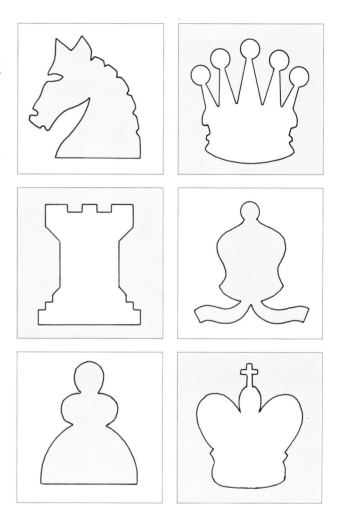

Full-size patterns for chess pieces.

3. Attach the grid to your cutting mat with pieces of sticky tape. Position all the squares and pieces (as they will be arranged on the shade) on a tray or worktop.

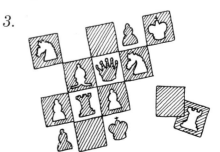

4. Position the clear adhesive-backed film, sticky side up, over the grid and secure with sticky tape. Replace the film backing, leaving the first row of squares visible. Carefully position each brown square and brown piece. When the first row is complete, lift the backing leaving the second row visible. Continue until the whole arrangement is complete, remembering to leave the three narrow gaps free.

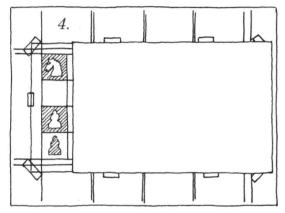

5. Trim the parchment to about 10mm (³/₈in) larger all round than the shade dimensions. Lay it on top of the clear adhesive-backed film and secure with sticky tape. Draw the brown lines for the top and bottom borders.

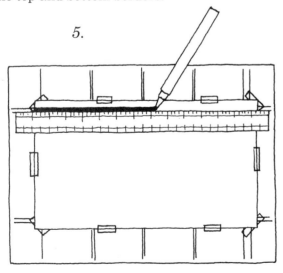

6. Using your steel-edged rule and the blunt edge of your knife, score the parchment down the middle of the narrow gaps and at the right-hand side (for the flap).

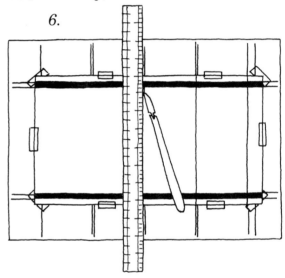

7. Cut the shade out. Turn it over and rub the brown paper pieces firmly to ensure adhesion. Use the end of your craft knife handle to get between the intricate bits.

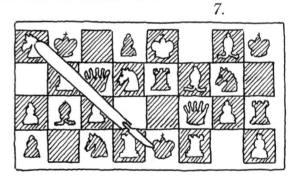

8. Crease the score lines as sharply as possible. Attach a strip of DSST to the flap and stick the sides together, with the flap on the outside of the shade.

Pyramid shade

This shade is made from a sheet of papyrus (from which the word
'paper' is derived), one of a dozen brought back from Egypt by a
colleague who has a passion for textured papers. Papyrus is created
from the stalk of a tall aquatic plant which grows on the banks of the
Nile. In ancient Egypt the reeds were split, woven at right angles,
and pressed, then left to dry in the sun. The sheets were then dressed
with a flour paste and polished with smooth stones.

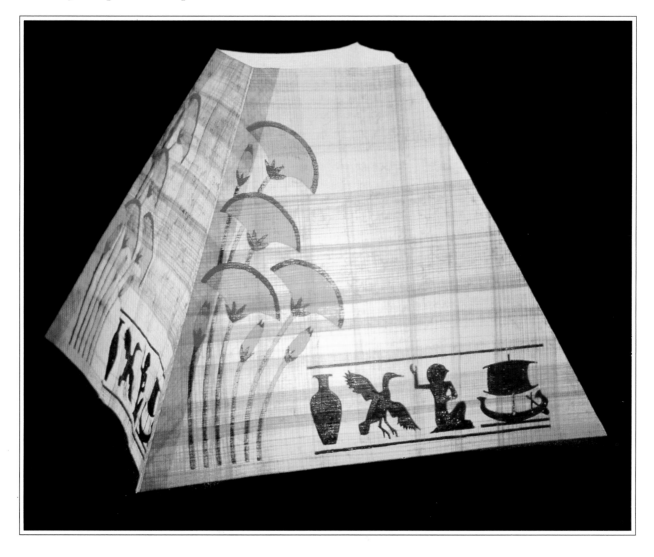

*To make the pyramid shade you will need: a 350 x 350mm (14 x 14in) square of
papyrus or similar patterned paper; some tracing paper; green, red and ochre
drawing inks; a tube of black gouache; a No. 2 or 3 paintbrush; and the
equipment given on page 4.*

Making the shade

1. Trace the full-size pattern and reproduce it four times on to the papyrus/paper. Carefully cut the sections out.

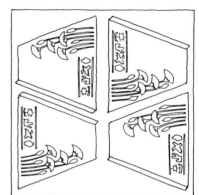

1.

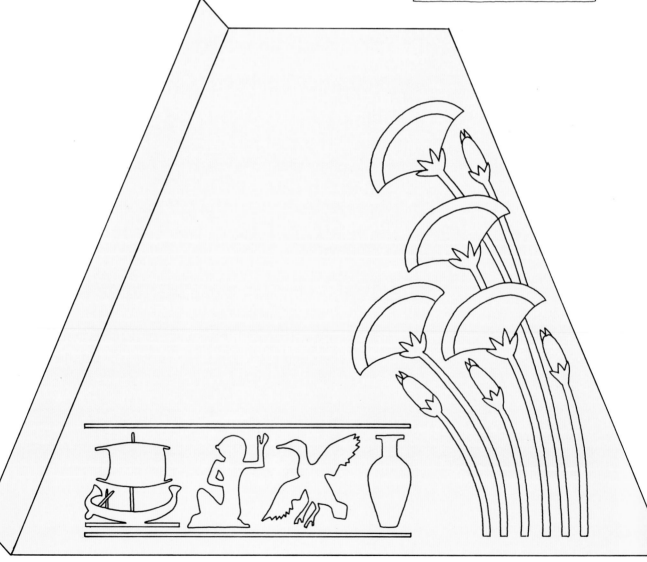

2. Lay one of the sections on to a piece of white paper, pencilled design facing down – you should be able to see the faint pencil lines through the papyrus. Carefully paint the hieroglyphic symbols with black gouache and the papyrus reeds with the inks. Repeat with the other three sections.

2.

3. When the paint/inks are completely dry lightly score the flap on each section.

3.

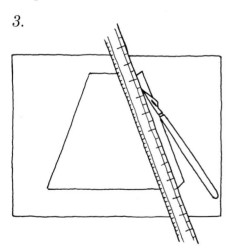

4. Stick strips of DSST down each flap then join the four sections together.

Note When lighting the shade, position the candle right in the centre of the shade, directly below the opening.

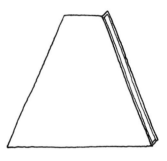

4.

Papyrus is not usually sold in art and craft shops but may be available from specialist paper merchants. Any paper of similar colour with a linear texture would do as a substitute.

Lemon-tree shade

Stained-glass effects can be achieved using transparent glass paint on acetate. The opaque background of this lemon-tree shade, which gives a nice contrast to the sharp, transparent colours of the tree, was made by mixing white with tiny amounts of blue, green and orange. Two sides of this four-sided shade are left solid to give strength and to allow the candlelight to reflect the whiteness of the two sides.

To make the lemon-tree shade you will need: an A3 (12 x 16¹/₂in) sheet of mounting board (black one side, white the other); an A4 (8¹/₄ x 12in) sheet each of acetate, tracing paper, plain white paper and thin white card; eight coloured transparent glass paints; glass-paint solvent; No. 2 paintbrush; black poster paint; small mixing palette; black felt-tipped pen; lighter fuel and cotton wool (commercial art clean is similar to lighter fuel but rather more expensive); and the equipment given on page 4.

Making the shade

1. Cut the four pieces of the frame from the mounting board. The two solid sides measure 80 x 190mm (3¹/₈ x 7¹/₂in). The two frames are 120 x 190mm (4³/₄ x 7¹/₂in). Draw a 20mm (³/₄in) border all round the two frames and cut out the centre portion. Using the black marker, blacken all the side edges of each of the four pieces.

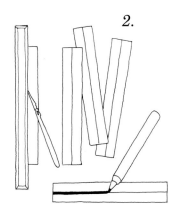

1.

2. Cut four 30 x 190mm (1³/₁₆ x 7¹/₂in) strips of thin white card. Lightly score a line exactly down the centre of each strip with the blunt edge of your knife. Using the black marker again, draw a 3mm (¹/₈in) wide line to cover the scored line.

2.

3. Cut four more pieces of the card, two at 19 x 76mm (³/₄ x 3in) and two at 19 x 119mm (³/₄ x 4¹¹/₁₆in). Stick a strip of DSST on the back of each.

4. Stick strips of 14mm (⁹/₁₆in) wide DSST down the sides of each of the frames (white side facing). Cut two pieces of acetate a little larger than the frames, clean both sides with lighter fuel and cotton wool and carefully attach the acetate to the frames. Trim away the excess so that the acetate is flush with the frame. Stick strips of DSST, the same width as before, down each side of the frames. Do not remove the backing.

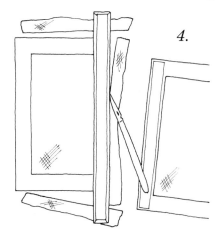

4.

5. Trace the design (overleaf) on to tracing paper twice. Lay the tracing on to a piece of white paper and secure with tape. With the white side facing, secure each frame over the tracing.

5.

6. Mix some black poster paint in your palette. The consistency should be wet, smooth and thick. Follow the outline of the designs. The first application will be streaky so repaint when the first coat is dry. (Practise on a spare piece of acetate first, until your line is steady and confident.)

6.

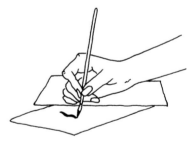

Always have a clean sheet of paper to rest your hand on while working on acetate – natural skin oils prevent the paint from being properly applied. Paint should be applied liberally, flooding it gently between the black outlines (black poster paint), rather than the usual method of painting with brush strokes.

7. Pour some white glass paint into the palette and add a little blue. Mix, then carefully flood the top area of both designs – take the paint up to the strips of DSST. Continue working down the fields, adding more white and specks of green, orange or blue to the original colour. Clean your brush with solvent then paint the leaves, carefully flooding both green and blue into each leaf shape. Repeat with brown for the trunk and yellow for the lemons, leaving a clear highlight at one side of each lemon. Leave the pieces to dry for two hours.

7.

8. Crease the four strips (corners) which have been scored. Remove all the DSST backing from the various pieces. Stick two corners to each frame, then the two longest of the four strips to the top of each frame.

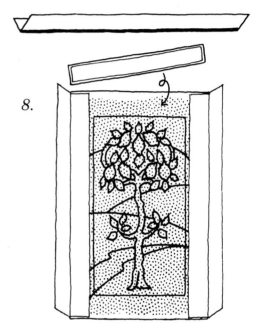

8.

9. Stick the two solid pieces to the frames, then the two shorter strips to the top of each solid piece. The shade is now complete.

9.

Spider's web

The rose outside my kitchen window was intended to ramble gently round the frame, giving a wistful, country-cottage feel to our suburban house. However, it had other ideas, one of which was to grow directly across the window, blocking out all light and encouraging strange insects. One morning I woke early and came down to find the most exquisite spider's web, hung with generous drops of dew . . . the inspiration for this candle-shade.

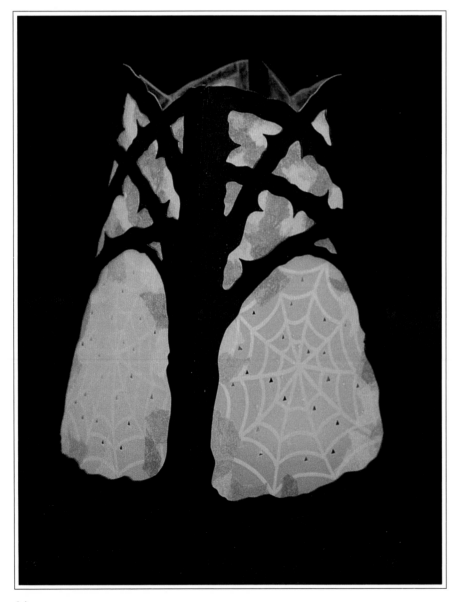

To make the spider's-web shade you will need: an A3 (12 x 16¹/₂in) sheet each of sturdy black paper, drafting film and clear acetate; an A4 (8¹/₄ x 12in) sheet each of tracing paper and white paper; white Conté crayon (like chalk but harder); glue stick; three different green tissue papers; silver poster paint; No. 2 paintbrush; felt-tipped marker; lighter fuel and cotton wool (see page 40); sticky tape; and the equipment given on page 4.

Making the shade

1. Using the full-size pattern below, trace the two designs (a1) and (a2).

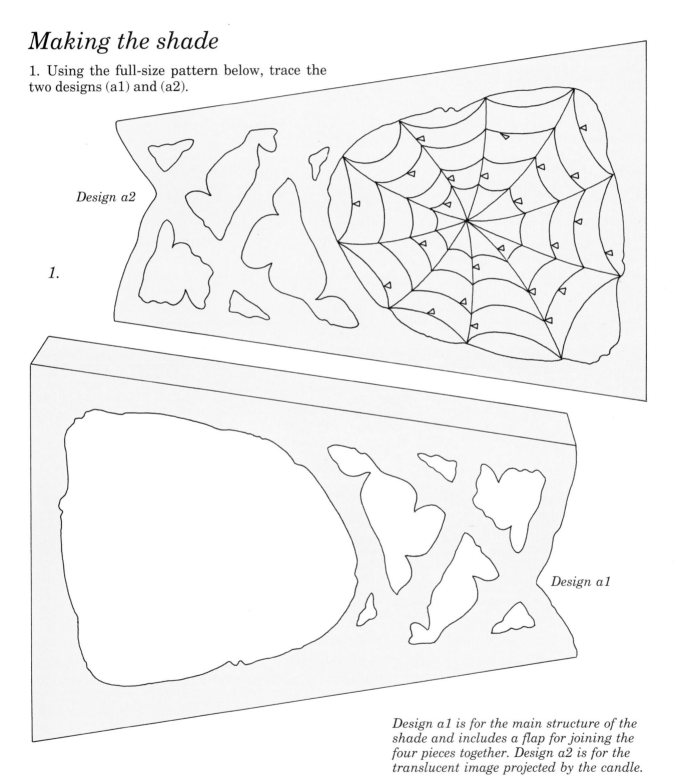

Design a2

1.

Design a1

Design a1 is for the main structure of the shade and includes a flap for joining the four pieces together. Design a2 is for the translucent image projected by the candle.

2. Turn tracing (a2) over and secure with pieces of sticky tape on to the white paper. Lay a piece of drafting film over the tracing and again secure with sticky tape. Lightly draw the outer edge (as a guide for cutting) and the small triangles – the dew drops.

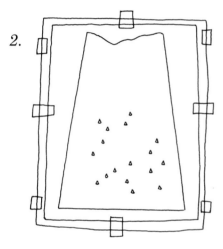

2.

3. Tear small, irregular pieces of tissue paper and using the glue stick overlap the pieces on to the areas between the branches, then add a few round the edge of the web.

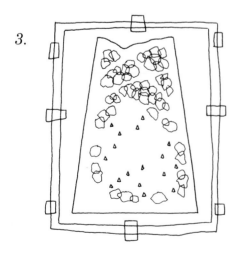

3.

4. Remove the drafting film and, using your knife, cut out the little dew drops (erase any

pencil marks). Cut out the whole shape. With right side facing, stick strips of DSST round the edges. Repeat the above instructions three more times, then leave the four pieces on one side.

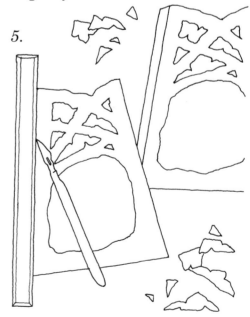

4.

5. Turn the tracing (a1) over and rub the pencil lines with Conté crayon, blowing excess dust away. Lay the tracing on the black paper, secure with sticky tape and trace the design four times. Carefully cut out the inner sections, then the whole pieces. Lightly score the flaps with the blunt edge of your knife.

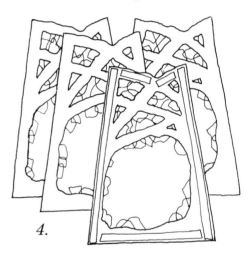

5.

6. Turn each piece over and stick a few small strips of DSST along the branches. Carefully attach the drafting film, positioning it just in from the edge. (The side on which you stuck the tissue should be facing.) Repeat with the three remaining pieces.

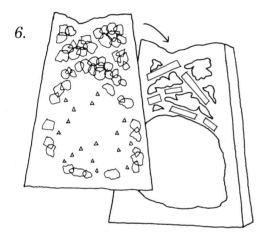

6.

7. Stick strips of DSST round the edges of the drafting film and on the branches as before – hold the piece up to the light to see where the branches are. With tracing (a2) still attached to the white paper, lay a piece of acetate over, securing with sticky tape. Wipe the acetate with lighter fuel and cotton wool. Draw round the outer edge of the design with the felt-tipped pen. Remove the acetate and cut out the shape. Carefully attach it to the drafting film.

7.

8. Lay the whole piece over the tracing. Secure with pieces of low-tack tape to prevent damage to the black paper. Carefully paint the web with silver paint. In daylight the web will look white; the lighted candle turns the web into a silhouette and the flickering flame pierces the little triangles to give the effect of dew caught by the sun. Repeat with the three remaining pieces.

8.

9. Stick strips of DSST down the flaps of each piece, right side facing, then join the four together.

Index